A Celebration of Autumn

DAVID ADAM

'A man who has lost his sense of wonder is a man dead.'

William of Thierry (1085–1148)

SPCK

Published in Great Britain in 2005

Society for Promoting Christian Knowledge
36 Causton Street
London SW1P 4ST

British Library Cataloguing-in-Publication Data
A catalogue record for this book is available from the British Library.

ISBN 0–281–05716–8

1 3 5 7 9 10 8 6 4 2

Designed and typeset by Monica Capoferri
Printed in Belgium

INTRODUCTION

Autumn is a time for joy and celebration. The bountiful goodness of creation, in the fruits of another year, calls to all our senses. Come, taste and see how good is the Lord. Come, smell the harvested field or the ripened apples. Come, touch the fruit. Look at the colours, experience new landscapes with widening vistas. This is a time for appreciating what is around us and what we have achieved. It is also a time for changing schools, going to college or university, beginning work. Autumn and its harvest often bring a reward for our labours. As the earth bears fruit we also grow and mature, we develop and realize new talents. Autumn is not so much a time to quantify and measure but to rejoice in who we are and what is around us.

It is a privilege if we can go out and collect apples, pears or plums. The hedgerows provide us with brambles, crab apples, hips and haws, with rowans and sloes: all can be stored as jellies or wines. In the fields there are mushrooms for those who know what is what. The fields are being harvested and crops stored for the year ahead. Here is life in abundance. It is time to give thanks and appreciate the wonder of life and creation.

Autumn begins as the nights grow darker and stars reappear in the evening sky. For me the evening of 31 August is the beginning: the night that marks the death of Aidan and the vision of angels by Cuthbert. We will see neither stars nor angels if we do not look for them. All of September, October and November make 91 days and constitute a quarter of the days of the year.

Autumn is a season of colour and contrasts. Bright days give way to fog. The glory of the autumn wood is suddenly stripped bare. It is a season of death and promised rebirth. It is the time of harvest and of bare fields. All is caught up in change, fecundity and decay. Autumn speaks of the generosity of God and shows the wonder of his creation.

Sometimes it is hard to trust the God who lays bare, who calls for loss and diminishment. It is a time for trust and for faith for it is truly the seedtime. Again and again we learn that dying is necessary for renewal; through breakdown and burial comes new life. Autumn is a time to praise God who makes all things new.

One of my favourite autumn moments comes from Julian of Norwich, who was the first woman of letters, writing at the time of Chaucer and of Joan of Arc. Standing with something like a hazelnut in her hand, Julian says:

'He showed me in my palm a little thing as round as a ball about the size of a hazelnut. I looked at it with the eye of understanding and asked myself:

'"What is this thing?"

'And I was answered, "It is everything that is created."

'I marvelled that it could last, for I thought it might have crumbled to nothing, it was so small.

'And the answer came into my mind, "It lasts and ever shall because God loves it." And all things have their being through the love of God.

'In this little thing I saw three truths. The first is that God made it. The second is that God loves it. The third is that God looks after it.

'What is he indeed that is maker and lover and keeper? I cannot find words to tell. For until I am one with him I can never have true rest nor peace.'[1]

1 From *Revelation of Divine Love*, Chapter 5

THERE IS HOPE FOR ME

God loves small things
He made them all
And he cares for them.
He truly loves nuts
Hazelnuts and cobnuts
Walnuts and chestnuts
Coconuts and peanuts
He loves you and me.
He made the planets
Sun, moon and stars
The earth and all on it
Yet God loves nuts
For he loves you and me.
God created us all
God keeps us all
God redeems us.
He is with all and in all
He is our keeper
Protecting us from evil
Shielding us from harm.
God loves small things
God loves nuts
He loves you and me.

THE DAWN

The dawn does not break
It caresses sleepless minds
It soothes the frightened child
Who was crying in the night

The dawn does not break
It fingers leaves on trees
Warms dew covered rabbits
The hedgehog under the leaves

The dawn does not break
Sensuously sliding on slopes
Silently slithering through streets
It comes with the greatest of ease

HARVEST MOMENT

The world has turned to gold
Barley fields with sensual hair
Holding the warmth of summer
And all the richness of days past
The sun and rain the soil and toil
In the seeds awaiting the harvest
Or yet another Lady of Shalott
To stand among the grain dreaming
Tears in her eyes, love in her heart
Sharing in a moment's beauty
Before the combine and tractor
Take the fruit of this year away

HURRAY* FOR THE HARVEST

Hurray for the harvest
For the sun and the rain
For the growth of the grain
For the richness of soil
For the outcome of toil

Hurray for the harvest
For combine and trailer
For tractor and baler
For grain silo and store
For all gathered once more

Hurray for the harvest
Of mind and insight
Of talent and might
Of love and of care
For growth everywhere

*'Hurray' is used here as a praise to God. I like to think that the word comes to us from the Gaelic *Ho Rí* which is 'Hail to the King'

LOVING

Autumn is a great time for loving: to discover that the world calls for our love and our respect. This is the world God made and he loves it. There is nothing in this world that is not worthy of love and awe. We need to learn to let this world touch us, to break in upon us, to tug at the heart. Once we allow this 'other' world to touch us we will be transformed. Autumn is a wonderful season to take time out and discover the uniqueness of each leaf and flower. Take to heart the words of Fyodor Dostoevsky:

'Love all God's creation, the whole of it and every grain of sand in it. Love every leaf, every ray of God's light. Love the animals, love the plants, love everything. If you love everything, you will perceive the divine mystery in things.'[1]

The great 'Other', who is God, offers his love to us through the world. God comes to us through his creation. If we are insensitive to the world around us, we will not be aware of our God. If we do not love the world, how can we begin to love its creator?

Let us not be preoccupied with another world when God has given us this one. This is the world God has made, this is the world God loves and this is the world in which he has placed us. Too often the revelatory powers of the earth and its creatures go unnoticed. The Church in Celtic lands talked of the three Scriptures: the New Testament, which cannot be fully understood without awareness of the Old Testament; the Old Testament, which cannot be understood without the Primary Scripture; the Primary Scripture, which is all of God's creation. It is sad that so many of us have become illiterate when it comes to reading the world. We need to regain a sense of awe and of love of life in the world about us.

'We need nothing but open eyes to be ravished like the Cherubims.'[2]

1 From *The Brothers Karamazov*, Book 6, Chapter 3
2 Thomas Traherne *Centuries*, Book 1, Section 37, Faith Press, 1960

SHARED MEMORIES

Come wander through the leaves
Through the tunnel of summers gone
Hand in hand down lanes of our youth
To moon and stars that gave lovers light
Entwined in each other, we walk as one
Up into the dancing of Northern Lights
Past quivering sheep in brackened fields
There is a star trapped in the dark water
And a mysterious owl piercing the night
Higher still upon the fox calling moors
We saw Orion and a shooting star
I made a wish then, it was a secret
But it was fulfilled for here you are

A SEA CHANGE

More than leaves fall
Countries, empires, people
Come to autumn and winter
Spiralling down from their heights
To become one with the ground
Compost and seed for the future
Renewing the face of the earth
Nothing on earth is ever truly lost
All goes through a sea change
Everything has tides and seasons
And in their present fall are seeds
The gifts and promises of new life
Every molecule knows it can become
Part of what it has never been before
Creator, with a wonderful precision
Seeding the world. Let us adore

SEEDS

In this seed
I made a flower
And that flower
Made a garden
And that garden
Delighted a couple
And that couple
With a seed
Made a child
And their child
Took some seeds
And made a loaf
And in that loaf
I did dwell
Who took a seed
And made a flower
And set a garden
For them to dwell

COME AWAY

Where the leaves are deep and crisp
And more are dropping from the tree
Where we get a glimpse of the sea
That's the place for you and me

Where the owl sits on the branch
And the squirrel keeps his pantry
Where the woodpecker hits the tree
That's the place for you and me

Where the hazelnuts are brown
And the sloes are in the hedges
Where conkers are falling free
That's the place for you and me

Where the stream is running clear
And the dipper is there to see
Where grey sheep are company
That's the place for you and me

MARY PONDERING

To be a mother
Without a husband
Born of my flesh
And of a dream
To remain chaste
Yet to birth a child
Too strange for Joseph
Gifts put in a drawer
No use for a child
The gold might be handy
The myrrh called upon
The incense, who knows?
He can work it out
Let him work like others
Take up a hammer and nails
Smooth wood with a plane
Learn not to go against the grain

A FISHERMAN WITH SOUL

Most of the time I make and mend
Whatever each day decides to send
A lobster pot or fishing net
A broken heart or a wireless set
Nothing is cast aside or lost
Everything is precious beyond cost
The old cast out cleaned and restored
The unwanted welcomed and adored

TRANSFORMATION

Could I slough off my skin
And slide away renewed?
A great trick to restore the body
Leaving the old at the roadside

Can this corpse-holding chrysalis
Take to wings and be a butterfly?
A most wonderful transformation
Exchanging the earth for the sky

How can this mud-crawling worm
Shimmer and shine as a dragonfly?
Turning from darkness and damp
giving light in the darkened wood

Is there hope for a body change
A resurrection morn trumpet call?
Let his mortal become immortal
My breakdown be a breakthrough

LOOKING AT THE *PIETÀ**

He rests now
Free from frustration and fear
No more rejection or abuse
No more measured cruelty
The whip will not hurt now
Thorns cannot pierce his mind
The warm heart is stilled

She bears the sorrow silently
The mindless agony
His body broken
But not his spirit
He will live on
Not just in hearts and minds
He will live beyond time
With the Father in love eternal

*On Holy Cross Day, 14 September 2004

VISION

How deep and mysterious is our world: wonder unfolds out of the most ordinary of things. Nothing at all is common or ordinary: flower, leaf, a drop of water all tremble with power and light. Vision is about seeing and how we see. Give your undivided attention to anything and it will grow before you revealing mystery upon mystery. Look closely at anything and it will show you depths that you have never seen before. If you stay there you will be overawed by its radiance and light. If this is not so, you have not looked long enough or closely enough. Those who have closed their hearts and minds through cares or carelessness miss the transforming power of the encounter. If we have not allowed ourselves to be enchanted, we have allowed something vital in our being to atrophy. God reveals himself to us through his creation.

I have often used the camera to teach young people to stop and look, to frame and focus on a single item and let it fill their vision. I have sent children around with cardboard tubes to peer through and see only one thing instead of a multitude, not to restrict their vision but that their vision may be increased. Too often we walk through a world of miracle and wonder and trample on all in our haste. We need to make the discovery that William Blake invites us to make:

To see a World in a Grain of Sand,
And Heaven in a Wild Flower:
Hold Infinity in the palm of your hand,
And Eternity in an hour.[1]

1 *Auguries of Innocence*, Book 2, lines 111–14

GOD'S LOST GIFTS

When our eyes were dimmed
So that we could not see
Beyond ourselves and our little world
You gave us the microscope
To discover the mystery of our being
To see beauty and harmony in all things
To learn that we belong to each other
You gave us the telescope
To see far beyond our little world
To rejoice in galaxies beyond galaxies
To fill our minds with awe and wonder
So we could bow before the majesty

We diminish it all in lack of vision
With myopic eyes, we analyse and count
We are not thrilled to the core
For there is a Black Hole within us
And sometimes that is all we can perceive

A DEEP WOOD

I lingered long in the wood
I slept: I dreamt: I woke
Was it night or day?
Leaf mould captures
And holds the mind
Above leaves shutter
And close out the sky
It is timeless here
And a restful brown
Which way do I go?
Where leads me to light?
Is it day now or night?
Hope and despair
Are together in the wood
One in eternal stillness
Of a man who has lost
His way

THE WORLD OF THE OTHER

By the end of October, we are moving into the long dark nights. Before the coming of electricity, it was a time to close down for the winter. It was a time for partial hibernation as for some of the animals. The Celtic peoples celebrated the festival of Samhain on the first of November. It was here the year ended and a new year began. All cattle that could not be overwintered were slaughtered and there was great feasting. The bone-fires, to get rid of the unwanted animal parts, burned brightly into the night. As a new year was about to start there was a sense that two worlds were drawing close together, that which had been and that which was to come. Both were close in the present. It is for this reason the Christian Church made 1 November All Saints' Day and 2 November All Souls' Day. We celebrate the unity of the Church in heaven and on earth.

With the belief that at this time our world and the next were brought much closer was the thought that the souls of the departed were also near at hand. It is important to realize that we are always leaving the old behind and entering the new. The present moment is where we are and there in us heaven and earth converge.

We seem to have lost sight of this other world or, as I prefer to call it, the world of the 'Other'. We have relegated it to a world of demons and dragons. Yet there is always the chance of the Other suddenly breaking into our awareness; the Other which is always there but waits to be revealed.

Throughout autumn, the great Other has been calling us and challenging us, if we have ears to hear, eyes to see and a heart to respond.

Anyone with a little sensitivity knows we belong to a world far greater than the one that is visible. We regularly join 'with angels and archangels and the whole company of heaven' not just in worship but in our daily living.

REMEMBRANCE

The sides of the path were red
Where the martyrs bled
With poppies

The pathway is bestrewn
With seeds that are sown
From poppies

And when this life is gone
Other seeds will carry on
Like poppies

ON LOOKING AT MILLAIS' *AUTUMN LEAVES*

Live life fully before the autumn
Make sure you blossom and flower
Let life be full of fruitfulness
Don't wait till the sunset hour
Gather leaves when you are older
Kick and dance in them when young
Don't be afraid! Be a little bolder!
You'll colour autumn when it comes
Rich or poor is not the measure
More important, to live in delight.
Let life itself be your treasure
Scatter the leaves! Enjoy the sight!

KICKING OLD LEAVES

Old leaves cannot show you a tree
Photographs cannot capture a sunset
Words will never tell you of me
Come meet me in my moving joy
In my ever shifting sorrow
See me when I am servile
Experience when I dominate
Do not give me a number
Or place me neatly on a file
That is not me, it may have been
Sometimes but it is not now
I am alive and ever changing
Unfolding and folding
Becoming and only rarely being

AUTUMN DIALECTIC

This is between world's time
The last rays of the sun fade
A day is coming to a close
Another about to begin
One is almost gone for ever
The other is coming to birth
Where do I belong at sunset?
To the past and the dead leaves
Or to tomorrow and its seeds?
I belong to this very moment
I belong to heaven and earth
I need not choose to enjoy one or the other
For both are mine

ILLUSTRATIONS

Tea in the Garden, 1921 by Ferdinand Achille Lucien Bivel (1888–1950), Gavin Graham Gallery, London, UK/Bridgeman Art Library.

On the Woodland Floor in October, 1998 (oil on board) by Raymond Booth (b. 1929), Private Collection, Fine Art Society, London/Bridgeman Art Library.

Fog on the Alster, 1894 (oil on canvas) by Ernst Wilhelm Heinrich Eitner (1867–1955), Hamburg Kunsthalle, Hamburg, Germany/Bridgeman Art Library.

Barley and Thistle, Clements Reach (oil on canvas) by Frederick John Pym Gore (b. 1913), Private Collection, Manya Fine Arts Ltd/Bridgeman Art Library.

Harvesting (oil on canvas) by Adolphe Joseph Thomas Monticelli (1824–86), Cuirlionis State Art Museum, Kaunas, Lithuania/Bridgeman Art Library.

Fig Harvesting in the South of France, c. 1900–20 (oil on canvas) by Blanche Camus (1884–1968), Private Collection, Archives Charmet/Bridgeman Art Library.

Janet's Steps, Cambridge, Massachusetts (collage with w/c on paper) by Christine McKechnie (b. 1943), Private Collection/Bridgeman Art Library.

Autumn Landscape, c. 1903 (oil on canvas) by Henri-Edmond Cross (1856–1910), Private Collection/Bridgeman Art Library.

In a Galloway Rose Garden by Hugh Munro (1873–1928), Whitford E. Hughes, London, UK/Bridgeman Art Library.

Landscape, Staffelsee in Autumn, c. 1923 (oil on canvas) by Gabrielle Munter (1877–1962), © DACS 2005/Private Collection/Bridgeman Art Library.

Alexandra (Meditation) (oil on canvas) by Dorothee Martin du Mesnil, Private Collection/Bridgeman Art Library.

Fishing Boats in a Northern Harbour by Adrian Paul Allinson (1890–1959), Waterman Fine Art Ltd, London, UK/Bridgeman Art Library.

Reflective Trees by Bob Broadley, reproduced courtesy of Pauntley Prints.

The Entombment, 1847–9 (oil on canvas) by (Ferdinand Victor) Eugene Delacroix (1798–1863), © Phoenix Art Museum, Gift of Mr Henry R. Luce/Bridgeman Art Library.

Blackberries and Holly with a Butterfly by Albert Durer Lucas (1828–1918), Christopher Wood Gallery, London, UK/Bridgeman Art Library.

In the Rain, 1882 (w/c on vellum) by Vincent Van Gogh (1853–90), Haags Gemeentemuseum, The Hague, Netherlands/Bridgeman Art Library.

Autumn Lake (oil on canvas) by James Hill (1930–2004), © The Sullivan Collection/Bridgeman Art Library.

Lighting Up Time, The Thames Embankment (oil on canvas) by Hugo Grenville (b. 1958), Private Collection/Bridgeman Art Library.

'La Palette Nous Voice', 1991 (oil on canvas) by Gilles Dupuis, Private Collection/Bridgeman Art Library.

Autumn Leaves, 1856 by Sir John Everett Millais (1829–96), © Manchester Art Gallery, UK/Bridgeman Art Library.

By the Lake (oil on canvas) by George F Henry (1858–1943), Private Collection, Bonhams, London, UK/Bridgeman Art Library.

The Twilight Moon, 1899 (oil on canvas) by Isaak Ilyich Levitan (1860–1900), State Russian Museum, St Petersburg, Russia/Bridgeman Art Library.